MEGASTARS™

PINK

LYN SIROTA

rosen publishing's
rosen central®

New York

Published in 2011 by The Rosen Publishing Group, Inc.
29 East 21st Street, New York, NY 10010

Copyright © 2011 by The Rosen Publishing Group, Inc.

First Edition

Library of Congress Cataloging-in-Publication Data

Sirota, Lyn A., 1963–
Pink / Lyn Sirota. – 1st ed.
    p. cm. – (Megastars)
Includes bibliographical references, discography, and index.
ISBN 978-1-4358-3577-1 (library binding)
ISBN 978-1-4488-2263-8 (pbk.)
ISBN 978-1-4488-2269-0 (6-pack)
1. Pink, 1979—Juvenile literature. 2. Singers—United States—Biography—Juvenile literature. I. Title.
ML3930.P467S57 2011
782.42164092–dc22
[B]
                                                    2010026865

Manufactured in the United States of America

CPSIA Compliance Information: Batch #W11YA: For further information, contact Rosen Publishing, New York, New York, at 1-800-237-9932.

On the cover: Pink's stage performances are an amazing combination of dance, singing, and even acrobatics.

CONTENTS

INTRODUCTION

What do you get when you mix a little rock, a little rhythm and blues, a little pop, and a whole lot of honesty, emotion, and edge? You get Pink, the over-the-top international superstar who blasted into stardom as a determined teenager.

Pink, whose given name is Alecia Beth Moore, was born in Doylestown, Pennsylvania. Doylestown is a small town just outside Philadelphia. While her musical tastes and interests take many forms, her artistry clearly reflects her outlook on life. Her music reflects both her personal story and the world in general.

"Although initially viewed as another face in the late-'90s crowd of teen pop acts, Pink (professionally known as P!nk) quickly transcended and outgrew that label with her combination of pop songcraft and powerhouse,

Pop artist Pink strikes a pose at the 2009 MTV Video Music Awards on September 13 in New York City. She arrived at the event with her husband, Carey Hart, in a fire truck.

rock-influenced vocals," said MTV.com. As a popular singer and song-writer, Pink is known for her "big voice" and her distinctive personality. She always tries to appear unique in her performances, songs, and image. With a visually tough exterior, Pink purposely encourages con-troversy in her songs. This leads her fans to think about the deeper message. There are "two sides to the woman born Alecia Beth Moore: the tattooed, tough, good-time girl who shot to fame on the back of party anthems such as 'Get This Party Started' and 'Feel Good Time,'" according to James Wigney of the *Sydney Sunday Telegraph*. Yet, when she reveals herself, "the serious, sensitive singer-songwriter has never been afraid to show her flaws, scars and views in songs such as 'Family Portrait,' 'Dear Mr. President' and 'Leave Me Alone (I'm Lonely),'" said Wigney. Pink is all about putting her edgy attitude out there. "It's about being alive and feisty and not sitting down and shut-ting up, even though people would like you to," Pink told Squidoo. com. So while she may, at times, sing the blues, she is totally Pink.

CHAPTER 1

THE EARLY YEARS

ink's parents are James Moore and Judy Kugel Moore. James was an insurance salesman and a Vietnam-era veteran. Judy was an emergency room nurse. Pink comes from a diverse background. Her mother is Jewish, and her ethnic background is Irish, German, and Lithuanian.

Pink, the youngest of two children, was born with a collapsed lung. She was often sick in her younger years with asthma, pneumonia, and ear infections. Her earliest memory was of her dad singing her to sleep in his rocking chair.

Pink's parents shared their love and enthusiasm for music with her. They introduced her to folk and soul music, and her father played guitar for fun. Her mother listened to artists such as Aretha Franklin, Dionne Warwick, Shirley Murdock, and Donny Hathaway. Her father played Bob Dylan, Don McLean, and Janis Joplin. Pink had the benefit of being exposed to different types of music from the start.

Pink's father instilled tough behavior in her early on. He taught her survival skills like how to fight, use weapons, and break wrists.

Pink's parents had a stormy marriage that ended in divorce when she was ten. Pink refers to her parents' relationship as "world war three." She said in her VH1 *Behind the Music* interview that she knew about divorce and what it meant before knowing about marriage. She says that her only escape from what was going on around her was in

Pink gives dad, James Moore, a squeeze at a party at The Pink Elephant in New York City. They were celebrating the release of her fourth album, I'm Not Dead.

her music. This early emotional experience would prove to be a garden of ripe material for Pink's songwriting later on.

ROCKY ROADS

Pink describes herself as being a "wild and difficult child" during her younger days, especially after her parents' divorce. Even though she had asthma, she experimented with smoking at an early age.

As a teen, Pink was interested in a variety of activities. Voice lessons early on helped her prepare for the gospel singing she did in church. She was the lead singer of a punk band called Middle Ground. While Pink was going to school, she was also going to rave and hip-hop clubs, playing field hockey, and doing gymnastics. Pink told VH1 during her *Behind the Music* interview that she never hung out with the jocks or the sheltered kids. Rather, she was the one causing the trouble, talking back, fighting, and skipping school.

TURNING PINK

There are several versions of how Alecia Beth Moore changed her name to Pink. Sources say that she took the nickname because of the character Mr. Pink in the Quentin Tarantino movie Reservoir Dogs. Others say the nickname came from an incident where she was embarrassed in summer camp after a boy pulled her pants down. And yet another version is that she took the nickname Pink as a result of her dyed pink hair. Alecia Beth Moore, now known professionally as Pink and alternatively as P!nk, said she's had the nickname since she was a little girl. It was during her two-year singing gig with the group Choice that she took the colorful nickname as her official stage name. "We're all Pink on the inside. We're all the same. It doesn't matter," she said in her VH1 Behind the Music interview.

Pink has her own views about the her name. In a 2008 MTV interview, Pink commented that "I thought the funniest part about being Pink was that I was sort of really aggressive and not how people relate to that color. I like the dichotomy. Pink is supposed to be a really soft, feminine color, and I have that, too. But mostly if you get in my face, I'll tell you exactly how I feel."

PINK

At Henson Studios, Pink performs "We Are the World 25 for Haiti" on February 1, 2010. More than eighty top music stars collaborated on a remake of the song to support Haitian earthquake relief.

At thirteen, Pink was working as a backup singer and dancer in Philadelphia clubs. She also began rapping with her friend Skratch's local rap group, Schools of Thought. At fourteen, Pink began experimenting with drugs, tattoos, and piercings and ran away from home on a regular basis. She was arrested for several misdeeds. She hung out with skateboarders at clubs and explored many music scenes from rock, punk, and rave to hip-hop, folk, R&B, and gospel. Music always remained an important part of her life. She started writing her own songs and performing at a local hip-hop hotspot, Club Fever. Pink wrote introspective and often dark poems that she turned into lyrics.

After her parents divorced, Pink lived with her mother. Pink compared their relationship to rams that were constantly butting heads. Her mother later kicked her out of the house because of Pink's wild lifestyle. After briefly living with friends and relatives, she moved in with her father. Later on, it was Pink's father who nurtured her and helped her with the many important decisions in her career. She was "daddy's little girl" and shares his wit and sarcasm. Pink also worked several jobs in minimum-wage places like Pizza Hut, McDonald's, Wendy's, and a gas station.

Pink's father explores his hard times as a soldier in the Vietnam War in the song "I Have Seen the Rain," which Pink used to perform with him at veterans' functions. "That's how I learned to harmonize—that's how I learned to love music," she told RollingStone.com. "I told him, I'm going to be famous one day, I'm going to buy you a motor home, and we're going to record that song."

James Moore said he first knew Alecia would be a star when he heard her sing Madonna's "Oh Father" at the Germantown Academy, outside of Philadelphia, when she was ten. "She sang, and you could have heard a pin drop in the place—and there was about 2,000 people there," Moore told RollingStone.com. "And right then, I knew it was definitely going to turn into something. She just absolutely wowed the crowd—they were standing, they were clapping, there was a standing ovation for her."

The hardest part of Pink's teen years, she told RollingStone.com, was the sense of nothing to look forward to. "My biggest [message] for young people now is that there's life beyond high school," said Pink. "You're grounded, your parents don't understand you, you hate them—yet it all goes away. The people that you think are the coolest are not going to be in ten years. So just hold on, it's going to be OK. And one day you're going to write all this down in a song."

EXPLOSIONS

After seeing Pink perform at age sixteen, an MCA Records representative asked her to try out for a rhythm-and-blues group called Basic Instinct, based in Atlanta, Georgia. Pink left high school and home to relocate to Atlanta to record a demo with the group. Afterward, she went back to earn her GED (high school equivalency diploma). Even though her audition was a success, the group disbanded. She was then invited to complete a three-singer lineup for a girl group called Choice, which was signed to LaFace Records in 1996. LaFace is a music label founded by the singer Babyface and the producer L. A. Reid. Pink had a two-year gig with Choice. But the group disbanded before they could record anything because of conflict over creative differences. Pink faced the same set of circumstances as before.

CHAPTER 2

PINK RAINBOW AFTER THE STORM

Even though it seemed bad luck was the norm for Pink, those explosive group experiences resulted in a rainbow after a bit of stormy weather. Pink's relationship with LaFace brought her to the attention of the label's cofounder, L. A. Reid. Because of that relationship, Reid paired her with the producer Daryl Simmons to write a chorus for the song "Just to Be Loving You." This rekindled Pink's interest in songwriting and gave her valuable experience. When Pink was approached to go solo, she knew it was going to be the toughest decision she'd ever make. Reid groomed Pink as a solo artist although they each had a different vision of the direction of her career. Pink believed that Reid wanted her to compromise who she was, but she held her ground. Reid and Pink continued to work together on her career even after he became president of Arista Records.

After Reid signed Pink to LaFace as a solo artist, he placed her in the studio with his partners, Babyface and Russell Simmons. They helped shape her solo debut. Pink cowrote half of the tracks on her solo debut, *Can't Take Me Home*, which sold more than half a million copies. On Billboard.com, Pink said, "The first album was a good introduction—it was testing the waters. No one knew who I was before 'There You Go.' They don't know that I was the lead singer of two punk bands and sang gospel in all-black churches. I wanted this album to represent that." Her debut album established Pink alongside

L. A. Reid and Pink pose at the 28th Annual American Music Awards afterparty. The awards were broadcast live from the Shrine Auditorium in Los Angeles, California.

teen pop singers such as Britney Spears and Christina Aguilera and R&B artists such as TLS and Kelis. Pink remained intent on differentiating herself from the pack with her rough image—cropped pink hair and tattoos. She became known as just Pink.

IDENTITY

Although Pink wrote many of the tracks on her debut album, she didn't actually like how they sounded. "There was no blood, sweat, or tears on my first album—and no emotional exchange between me and the musicians," she told London's *Daily Mail.* It was proof she could sing and sell records, but the album created some controversy over who Pink really was. One issue that arose among music buyers was her ethnicity. Pink told reporter T'cha Dunlevy of the *Montreal Gazette,* "That's part of the mystery of Pink. Nobody knows what I am. Everybody thinks I'm what they are. White people think I'm white, Spanish people think I'm Spanish.

Pink took a break from writing and recording to work on a remake of Patti LaBelle's "Lady Marmalade" with Christina Aguilera, Mya, and Lil' Kim. The song was featured on the soundtrack for the movie musical Moulin Rouge! and went to number one in both the United States and the United Kingdom. Pink was part of one of the biggest worldwide pop hits of 2001. This earned Pink, at age twenty-two, a Grammy Award for Best Pop Collaboration with Vocals. An accompanying video featured the quartet dressed in lingerie, with Pink as the flashiest member of the group. It placed number three on MTV's Total Request Live year-end countdown and exposed Pink's artistry to a completely different audience.

Some black people think I'm black. I don't really care. Just listen to my music." This misperception appealed to Pink, who enjoys challenging stereotypes. She told the *Atlanta Journal-Constitution*, "I'm sort of like a big mystery bag. Put your hand in, you never know what you're going to get. I like it that way. I like confusing and blurring lines." Perhaps the identity crisis will be the basis of her next album?

JUST PINK

Pink outgrew her teen pop act label with her pop songcraft and powerhouse vocals. At nineteen, she took hold of her career and broke away from the image that her handlers wanted her to develop. She hired Roger Davies as a manager and stood up to her record company so that she could create an album that reflected her personality and sound. Pink wanted to be more rock than polished R&B or pop. She told Robert Hilburn of the *Los Angeles Times*, "Everything in this business is designed to encourage you to play along. They know people are so hungry for stardom that they'll just follow the record industry game. I know

because I was ready to do anything when I started out. But I found that selling records wasn't enough. I told myself after the first record that I'd rather go back home and start all over again than be trapped in a one-dimensional world any longer."

"Lady Marmalade" ladies from left to right: Lil' Kim, Christina Aguilera, Pink, and Mya at the Metropolitan Opera House at Lincoln Center, New York City.

Teaming up with former 4 Non Blondes singer Linda Perry, Pink wrote half the songs for her second album, *Missundaztood*. Pink explained in an interview that she was at a photo shoot and discovered Perry's phone number in her makeup artist's phone book.

Pink performed with singer/songwriter Linda Perry at the Los Angeles Gay and Lesbian Center's "An Evening with Women" in May 2010. Perry invited Pink onstage to perform Perry's song "What's Going On."

Because Pink says she's nosy, she used the number and called Perry repeatedly, "stalking her" and leaving long messages on her answering machine. Perry was Pink's childhood idol, and Pink said Perry spoke her language. Perry finally told her she was crazy and that she should come over. Pink said their music making was "like two thunderstorms that waited a lifetime to combust."

"Instead of being pigeonholed into one genre, I wanted to go across the board and do everything," Pink said on Billboard.com. Her disco pop song "Get the Party Started," written by Perry, exploded onto the charts upon release. This album sold more than eight million copies worldwide. Despite L. A. Reid's blessing that he was going to give her the opportunity to fail, Pink had officially achieved her goal. She became an R&B/rock musician and rebel girl who connected with millions of fans.

HEART TO HART

After several years of relationships and romances with men such as rocker Tommy Lee, Pink proposed to motocross racer Carey Hart. During one of his motocross races, she stood in the pit and held up a pit board sign that read, "Will you marry me?" According to *Sunday Life*, Pink said that "usually a mechanic writes on it things like 'breathe,' 'relax,' or 'you're in fourth place.' He didn't see it on the first lap, but on lap three he basically took out another rider to get off the track and everyone in the stands was cheering. Then I told him to get back into the race—because I don't marry losers!" They got married on a beach in Costa Rica in 2006. Carey managed to bring everyone to tears with his four pages of sweet words for Pink during their beach wedding.

According to People.com, they later separated in 2008. Touring put a strain on their relationship, and Pink commented that she'd never failed so publicly. They would go for months without seeing

Motocross champion Carey Hart smiles at pop champion Pink. Despite the ups and downs in their relationship, as in any normal relationship, they choose to be together.

each other. In April 2009, they reunited and renewed their wedding vows in a ceremony in California the next month. Pink told *USA Today* shortly afterward, "We're better people now. There's something about me and Carey . . ." Hart told *People*, "We're rebuilding. You take a couple of steps backward to move forward." Pink told the *Huffington Post*, "We never really legally got divorced. Paperwork for both of us is really annoying. So we're choosing to be together. Our role models are Tim Robbins and Susan Sarandon and Kurt Russell and Goldie Hawn—people who just choose to be together every day because they want to be there. And labels have never been our thing, so we're just diving into that empty swimming pool, headfirst."

CHAPTER 3

FEARLESS

Pink's album, *Missundaztood,* produced several hit singles like "Get the Party Started" and "Just Like a Pill." The song "Family Portrait" became a worldwide hit and was about her parents' marital problems and their effects on her, seen from a child's point of view. At first it devastated her parents. They couldn't believe she was so public with private information. Yet, it brought their family together in a stronger bond afterward. It was difficult yet cathartic for her to sing, and it helped her repair her relationship with her mother. On PinksPage.com, her mom recalled, "I can remember talking about the song 'Family Portrait' in interviews and just crying. Each record got a little deeper and more cathartic than the last. Pink sang about herself, her rough teenage years, and her problems with her family and the music industry in an emotionally intense fashion."

In 2003, Pink released the album *Try This,* which featured a number of musical styles recorded mostly in her own home studio. The critics praised this release but also pointed out that it sounded similar to her second record but without the danger and radio-friendly hooks. A review in *Newsweek* said, "Thanks to boot-stomping tempos, hissing guitar, and rough-and-tumble melodies, the music finally matches Pink's acerbic lyrics and overall bad attitude." Even with many critics impressed, the first single, "Trouble," only reached number 16 on the Billboard Top 40 charts and was not much of a hit on the radio. Yet, this lead single gained Pink a second Grammy Award. She told

Pink poses with her platinum album Funhouse *in Rotterdam, Holland, on December 6, 2009. "Sober," a very deep, personal song on the album, topped the charts.*

Nekesa Mumbi Moody of the Associated Press, "I don't judge myself on how well my songs do at radio, or how much my album sells. A failure and a success is all how you look at it. I've been creative to my highest potential at this point of my life, and I'm super proud of myself for making it this far."

With the release of Pink's fourth album, *I'm Not Dead*, the number 1 single "Stupid Girls" was a social commentary about pop singers and actresses like Britney Spears, Paris Hilton, Lindsay Lohan, and Jessica Simpson. Pink told the *Daily Mail*, "It was more of a social commentary on these girls, who think they have to be stick thin and have the latest handbag." Pink commented that there is nothing wrong with this as long as you're doing it for yourself and not society. Her message to fans according to Billboard.com is that "you don't have to be a

Pink's creativity doesn't stop with singing, songwriting, dance, or gymnastics. In addition to her contribution to the film Moulin Rouge!, *Pink has appeared in minor roles in the films* Rollerball *(2002),* Charlie's Angels: Full Throttle *(2003), and* Catacombs *(2007). Pink was also supposed to play Janis Joplin in a movie about the singer, whose solo career lasted only a few years. Joplin was considered one of the greatest female singers in rock history. According to* The Gospel According to Janis *director Penelope Spheeris, "To see this girl bring Janis to life was profound." The girl is Pink, who was cast in the lead role. This film would have been Pink's acting debut. Spheeris was so blown away by her screen test that deciding to cast her was a no-brainer. Spheeris also directed* Wayne's World *and* The Decline of Civilization *trilogy. Pink later pulled herself out of the running for this film.*

millionaire to be cool. You don't have to have the latest fashion. I was put on this Earth to make fun of myself and other people." The end of the video features a little girl choosing between two play activities, and she chooses playing sports over playing with Barbie dolls.

The singer also gets serious on the track "My Vietnam." Pink told Billboard.com, "It was just about life, but now it's taken on a whole new meaning." That is, a deeper meaning since September 11, 2001.

DEEP CRAFT

By sharing such intimate details about life and the world, Pink said it is "like standing naked in front of an auditorium full of people." She hopes her songs will touch someone else. "If I can help somebody else out by doing it, then so be it." However uncomfortable her songs might be for her and her family, they can be comforting and inspirational to fans. While promoting *Missundaztood* and talking about her pain, she received a letter from a girl who was suicidal and had not spoken with her parents in seven years. After listening to "Family Portrait," according to the *Sydney Sunday Telegraph*, she didn't want to kill herself anymore and reopened her relationship with her parents. Pink told the *Sydney Sunday Telegraph*, "That's when I realized it's hard, it's uncomfortable at times, it's even annoying at times, but I am never going to do it any other way because it's worth it to people."

"Aside from a few songs that are completely vulnerable for me," Pink told the *Huffington Post*, "when I am writing even my angry kind of 'So What,' for me, it's every emotion involved—I'm being sarcastic, I'm being silly, I'm being angry, I'm all of these emotions, all at the same time, so I include them in my songs. So it is still silly, it's still funny, I still have anger. It's really easy to just be right back there . . . I don't have a hard time transplanting myself straight back to that moment."

"You can't be creative when you're completely happy," Pink told RollingStone.com. "When I'm totally happy, I have no thoughts in my head. If life is a big search, then you're never content, you're always looking. And if you're always looking, then you're not completely happy."

Pink has shared that she chose her life and all its obstacles and challenges, and it is all of that which has allowed her to write the songs she writes and not be afraid of the pain.

FUNHOUSE

With her fifth studio album, Pink got even more revealing. The title *Funhouse*, according to Pink, is a metaphor for life and love. She told the *Sydney Sunday Telegraph*, "This is my most vulnerable album to date." She said she had no problem talking openly about the split from her husband, Carey Hart, during this time. He is the subject of some of the songs on the *Funhouse* album. Writing and singing about her breakup was therapeutic for Pink. "It's like letting down the armour

During the first night of her European Funhouse tour, Pink performs in Nice, France, in February of 2009. In her classic, over-the-top style, no one can sing it better.

and admitting I'm human, I'm a girl," Pink explained on her Web site, PinksPage.com. "I look at life like a carnival. Clowns are supposed to be happy, but they are really scary. . ." She admits that it felt as scary as it felt great to reach new depths of vulnerability on tracks like "Please Don't Leave Me," a painfully honest love song disguised by upbeat, cheerful instrumentation. In "Glitter in the Air," Pink asks a lot of questions such as "Have you ever looked fear in the face and said I just don't care?" and "Have you ever hated yourself for staring at the phone?" Pink admitted, "I still don't have some of the answers to the questions I pose on this record. I'm still figuring it all out."

Pink's world tour for the release of this album added another level of talent to her skills: athlete. "Early in the show," according to the *New York Times*, "she casually did a gymnastic flip onto a couch between songs. And near the end, Pink belted 'Get the Party Started' from overhead at the arena, hanging upside-down from a trapeze by one knee." The Funhouse tour was a circus-themed extravaganza with dancers, aerialists, funhouse mirrors, and giant, inflatable clowns. It was described by the *New York Post* as an event that was as visually stunning as a Las Vegas Cirque du Soleil show. Pink, described as frisky and flamboyant, didn't lip-synch, even when she was skipping down a long runway in high heels. For her finale, she chose the song "Glitter in the Air" and rose up suspended below a team of aerialists who performed slow-motion Cirque du Soleil poses. The apparatus dipped her into a tank of water and she emerged with it pouring off of her, glittering in the spotlight. Pink told Oprah Winfrey on her show on February 5, 2010, that when she performed this song during the Grammy Awards, she wanted to "get all the famous people wet." Pink launched into a series of aerial acrobatics. All the while, she sang about taking chances and finding joy. During her interview on *Oprah*, she told the audience that she, in fact, sings better upside-down.

Pink earned two Grammy Award nominations for Best Pop Vocal Album for *Funhouse* and Best Female Pop Vocal Performance for her hit single "Sober." She performed "Glitter in the Air" at the Grammy Awards in January 2010. Pink released *Funhouse Tour Live in Australia*, which captures her performances and had the critics talking. The *New York Times* said that "even in an era of escalating pop spectacle, Pink's Funhouse tour is going to be hard to top . . . Onstage she was a down-to-earth superwoman." The *Chicago Tribune* said, "Pink combines showmanship with her powerhouse vocals, for an evening worth the price of admission."

CHAPTER 4
COMMITTED TO THE CAUSE

Pink is deeply committed to a number of issues and causes and speaks openly about them. At a young age, Pink was exposed to community service when she assisted with fund-raisers for Vietnam veterans. Her father started up a Bucks County chapter of Vietnam veterans. This, she told VH1 in her *Behind the Music* interview, gave her a solid center for who she now is.

Music helps Pink share her opinions about animal abuse, self-esteem, war, and politics. Her 2007 song release, "Dear Mr. President," was a social commentary on George W. Bush, who was president at the time. She even used her own money to buy airtime so this song could be played on major radio stations across the country despite the controversial words. Pink said that her intent was not to randomly insult and offend people but to inspire communication and raise awareness. Often artists will avoid controversy and "keep the peace" so that they don't offend fans. Pink insists she won't stay quiet just so she can make money.

Through her close association with People for the Ethical Treatment of Animals (PETA), Pink has become an outspoken campaigner on many controversial issues involving the treatment of animals. According to PETAkids.com, Pink never misses a chance to speak out for animals.

On the topic of herself, Pink told the *Bucks County Courier* that "Pink isn't just a color—it means something. We need to find a cure

New York councilman Tony Avella chats with Pink in front of a billboard with her picture. She partnered with People for the Ethical Treatment of Animals (PETA) to introduce legislation that bans horse-drawn carriages.

for breast cancer. I've been lucky, but you know of people who have been diagnosed with breast cancer. Just look in the musical community and you have Sheryl Crow and Melissa Etheridge. That hits pretty close to home. Hopefully, we can find the cure to breast cancer soon and all the awareness about it helps."

Pink contributes to charitable organizations such as the Human Rights Campaign, which ensures equal rights for lesbian, gay, bisexual, and transgender individuals, and the ONE Campaign, which fights AIDS and poverty. She also contributes to Prince's Trust, which provides funds and support to assist people starting businesses; the New York Restoration Project; and Save the Children, which works to create change for disadvantaged children in forty-two nations.

OUT THERE

The nature of Pink's writing style is deep, honest, and personal. She makes the choice to put her personal issues, struggles, and views out there for the public. This takes an extraordinary level of confidence and makes Pink an interesting artist to watch. Her style also prompts fans to pay attention to the lyrics of her songs.

When Pink performed in Dubai—a state in the United Arab Emirates—she received ten pages of instructions on exactly what she could and could not do and wear. She could not perform "Dear Mr. President," yet she could wear a miniskirt. While in the elevator of her hotel in Dubai, she was wearing a miniskirt and sleeveless tank top that offered a view of her tattoos. According to TheNational.com, she immediately felt disapproval:

> Perhaps her fellow travelers had noticed the two red ribbons on the back of either thigh or the adage "What Goes Around Comes Around" inscribed on her wrist. But who couldn't be forgiven for raising an eyebrow at the one which quotes

As a nominee for Best Female Pop Vocal Performance for "Stupid Girls," Pink arrives at the 49th Annual Grammy Awards in Los Angeles. "Stupid Girls" is from the I'm Not Dead album.

Ecclesiastes 3:4 below the tattoo of a bulldog: "A time to weep, a time to laugh, a time to mourn, a time to dance. Sleep in peace my darling. I love you." The dog in question was Elvis, a present from Lisa Marie Presley and one of Pink's best friends.

The dog drowned in her swimming pool in 2007. Pink told TheNational. com she was devastated.

UNDERRATED

Some say Pink is the world's most underrated superstar. Specifically, James Montgomery of MTV.com described her as "a fabulously fearless pop artist, as comfortable taking on George W. Bush as she is hanging like a bat from the rafters of Radio City" in New York City. "She is a deceptively good singer." Even given this, if the public was questioned about who the top pop stars are, Pink's name would probably not even make the top five. Perhaps this is because she is not a pure pop star, since she spans many music categories. Said Montgomery, "Pink is kind of a rock star. She is kind of a party girl. She is kind of an R&B diva too (or, at least she used to be). And she's created a particular niche in the pop universe that somehow manages to combine all those things."

Pink has sold more than thirty million albums worldwide and landed many Billboard hits, and her Funhouse tour was the ninth highest grossing act of the year. Montgomery believes Pink is "set up for the long haul. She's a career artist, unafraid to take risks and deal with the repercussions, and as such, she'll still be here long after her contemporaries have disappeared. Then again, if she keeps dangling upside down, she might not make it that long. And, really, she shouldn't have to go to such lengths (or heights) to be loved. Though, now that I think of it, she wouldn't be Pink if she didn't."

After the Dubai show, Pink met a woman, said TheNational.com, who told her that "it had been her 15 minutes of freedom." She was shaking from the experience. Pink commented that "the call to prayer is one of the most beautiful things I've ever heard. You don't get that in Vegas."

ON THE COVER

Pink was featured on the cover of the January/February 2010 *Women's Health* magazine. She told the *Women's Heath* team that she worked hard for her body. "It's about balance—you've got to make yourself happy. You can't be all work and no play." Pink tours with her bodyguard, who tells the magazine, "She can take care of herself." Pink's buff body is showcased in her formfitting concert attire when she is doing her upside-down stunts and dangling by one leg from a trapeze. Her consistent workout, she said, is what restored her confidence. She told *Women's Heath* that working out helps her feel strong, healthy, and good about herself. She also watches her diet very carefully.

When asked if it is hard being away from home for so long when she is on tour, she told *Women's Health*, "I'm a performer. I sing my life. It's like I'm having group therapy 350 days a year, and the people who come to the show get that, and they're there for that—whether it's to be lifted up, or to be lifted out, or just entertained or inspired, or to feel not so alone. That's how I feel when I'm singing my songs: These people are all going through the same things I am. I'm not alone either. I'm getting something out of it too."

OVER THE TOP

Any intention of toning herself down? Doubtful. One of her performances in Ireland even brought a storm of protest. Some families walked out of her concert saying that some of the things that happened

Pink enjoys a break from performing while in Sydney, Australia. During her tour, she sang a stunning rendition of "Bohemian Rhapsody" that showcased her amazing range of vocal capabilities.

onstage were too explicit and that she went way overboard. Some felt her language was offensive. Pink's response, according to *Sunday Life*, was, "If they thought that way out, they ain't seen nothing yet."

It seems Pink won't ever hesitate to share her thoughts on numerous topics. Her father used to tell her that if you're always honest you may not have many friends, but you won't have any enemies because they'll know exactly where you're coming from. Her honesty and strong commitment to every cause brings her a massive fan base who listens whether she is speaking or singing. Pink told CNN.com, "I'd rather fall down for what I believe in and for what makes me tick. Is that smart? Who knows. Might not be. But there's still some fear in me—I want to be understood. I want to be heard." Pink has never been afraid to speak her mind, bare her soul, and share her deepest feelings in her songs. As she says on her Web site, "I have no choice. It's what I do."

TIMELINE

1979 Alecia Beth Moore is born in Doylestown, Pennsylvania.

1996 Pink joins all-girl group Choice.

2000 She officially becomes "Pink" professionally, goes solo, and cowrites half the tracks on her debut, *Can't Take Me Home*.

2001 Pink gets a Grammy for her work on "Lady Marmalade," a song on the soundtrack for *Moulin Rouge!*, a movie musical; Pink teams up with former 4 Non Blondes singer Linda Perry to write the songs for her second album, *Missundaztood*.

2002 Pink has a role in the movie *Rollerball*.

2003 Pink releases the album *Try This*. The first single, "Trouble," gains her a second Grammy Award; she has a role in the movie *Charlie's Angels: Full Throttle*.

2006 Pink and Carey Hart marry on the beach in Costa Rica; she releases her fourth album, *I'm Not Dead*, featuring the single "Stupid Girls," a social commentary.

2007 Pink has a role in the movie *Catacombs*.

2008 Pink releases her fifth album, *Funhouse*, and performs in a world tour.

2010 Pink is nominated for two Grammy Awards and performs "Glitter in the Air" during the ceremony.

DISCOGRAPHY

ALBUMS

2000 *Can't Take Me Home*
2001 *Missundaztood*
2003 *Try This*
2006 *I'm Not Dead*
2008 *Funhouse*

SINGLES

2000 "There You Go"
2001 "Don't Let Me Get Me"
2001 "Family Portrait"
2002 "Just Like a Pill"
2003 "Trouble"
2003 "God Is a DJ"
2006 "Stupid Girls"
2006 "U & Ur Hand"
2007 "P!nk Remix"
2008 "So What"

Pink poses with her 2006 album *I'm Not Dead*. Pink has said that the album is about "being alive and feisty and not sitting down and shutting up."

ACERBIC Bitter or sharp in tone, taste, or manner.

CATHARTIC Producing a feeling of being purified emotionally, spiritually, or psychologically as a result of an intense emotional experience or technique.

COLLABORATION The act of working together with one or more people in order to achieve something.

COMMENTARY A record of events usually written by someone who participated in them.

CONTROVERSY Disagreement or strong opinions on or about a topic.

DECEPTIVELY In a way that misleads.

DEVASTATED To shock or upset someone greatly.

DICHOTOMY A separation into two divisions that differ from each other.

DISBANDED To break up as a group or organization.

EXTRAVAGANZA A lavish or spectacular event.

FLAMBOYANT Showy and striking.

GIG A musical performance.

GOSPEL Music that expresses spiritual belief, particularly in Christianity.

HARMONIZE To sing or play a musical instrument in a pleasing way.

INTROSPECTIVE Reflective and looking inward.

MINIMUM WAGE The minimum salary that an establishment must pay an employee by law.

MOTOCROSS A motorcycle race or the sport of racing motorcycles over a rough course.

NICHE A position or activity that suits someone's talents and personality.

PIGEONHOLED To be assigned to a category without a great deal of thought.

RAVE A type of music that is electronically synthesized.

REKINDLED To revive a feeling or interest.

RELOCATE To move away from the place where you live.

REPERCUSSIONS Something that happens after an action that is unforeseen.

SARCASM To make fun of or mock something.

STEREOTYPE A commonly held belief about a specific type of individual.

THERAPEUTIC Describes something used in the treatment of somebody's health.

TRANSCENDED To go beyond something in quality or achievement.

TRANSGENDER A person attempting or appearing to be the opposite sex.

TRAPEZE An aerial apparatus consisting of a short metal bar hung by ropes or metal straps.

VETERAN A person who has had long service in the military.

VULNERABLE Open to physical or emotional harm.

WIT Humor.

Broadcast Music, Inc.
320 West 57th Street
New York, NY 10019-3790
(212) 586-2000
Web site: http://www.bmi.com
Broadcast Music, Inc., collects license fees from businesses that use
   music and distributes the money as royalties to songwriters,
   composers, and music publishers.

Canadian Recording Industry Association
85 Mowat Avenue
Toronto, ON M6K 3E3
Canada
(416) 967-7272
Web site: http://www.cria.ca
The Canadian Recording Industry Association is a nonprofit group
   that represents Canadian companies that make and sell sound
   recordings.

Recording Academy/Grammy Foundation
3402 Pico Boulevard
Santa Monica, CA 90405
(310) 392-3777
Web site: http://www.grammy.com
The Recording Academy recognizes musicians through the annual
   Grammy Awards. Its partner, the Grammy Foundation, promotes
   the contributions of recorded music to American culture.

Rhythm & Blues Foundation
P.O. Box 22438

Philadelphia, PA 19110
(877) 772-1514
Web site: http://www.rhythm-n-blues.org
The Rhythm & Blues Foundation is a nonprofit organization dedi-
cated to rhythm and blues music. It provides financial and
medical assistance, educational outreach, performance opportu-
nities, and archival activities. Its programs recognize artistic
contributions and excellence.

Rock and Roll Hall of Fame and Museum
1100 Rock and Roll Boulevard
Cleveland, OH 44114
(216) 781-7625
Web site: http://www.rockhall.com
Through exhibits and education, the Rock and Roll Hall of Fame and
Museum works to preserve and promote the history and influence
of rock music.

Songwriters Association of Canada
26 Soho Street, Suite 340
Toronto, ON M5T 1Z7
Canada
(866) 456-7664
Web site: http://www.songwriters.ca
Through education and support, the Songwriters Association of
Canada works to help songwriters with both the business aspects
and the creative process of songwriting.

Songwriters Guild of America
209 10th Avenue South, Suite 321
Nashville, TN 37203
(615) 742-9945
Web site: http://www.songwritersguild.com

The Songwriters Guild of America works to protect the legal rights of songwriters and to provide education about songwriting and music.

Sony Music
Sony Music Entertainment Headquarters
550 Madison Avenue
New York, NY 10022
(212) 833-8000.
Web site: http://www.sonymusic.com
Sony Music is a worldwide leader in music entertainment, with recordings dating back to 1904. Labels under the Sony Music umbrella include Columbia, Epic, Jive, RCA, Sony Nashville, Legacy Recordings, Victor Records, and Sony Masterworks. Arista is a subsidiary.

WEB SITES

Due to the changing nature of Internet links, Rosen Publishing has developed an online list of Web sites related to the subject of this book. This site is updated regularly. Please use this link to access the list:

http://www.rosenlinks.com/mega/pink

FOR FURTHER READING

Bass, Lance. *Out of Sync: A Memoir*. New York, NY: Simon and Schuster, 2007.

Cabot, Meg. *Teen Idol*. New York, NY: HarperTeen, 2005.

Cohn, Rachel. *Pop Princess*. New York, NY: Simon and Schuster, 2004.

Friedman, Myra. *Buried Alive: The Biography of Janis Joplin*. New York, NY: Crown Publishing, 1992.

Harmel, Kristin. *When You Wish*. New York, NY: Delacorte Press, 2008.

Jones, Jen. *Becoming a Pop Star*. Mankato, MN: Capstone, 2008.

Niedzviecki, Hal. *The Big Book of Pop Culture: A How-To Guide for Young Artists*. Toronto, ON: Annick Press, 2007.

Tauber, Michelle. *Make Me a Pop Star*. New York, NY: Little, Brown Books for Young Readers, 2005.

BIBLIOGRAPHY

Aquilante, Dan. "Pink Outside the Box." *New York Post*, October 7, 2009. Retrieved November 12, 2009 (http://www.nypost.com/p/entertainment/music/pink_outside_the_box_y2rOXs4hrYhuiyRCqCTUhI).

Billboard.com. "Pink Insists She's M!ssundaztood." Retrieved November 19, 2009 (http://www.billboard.com/artist/pink/333418#/news/pink-insists-she-s-m-ssundaztood-1137483.story).

Boone, Mary. *Pink*. Hockessin, DE: Mitchell Lane, 2010.

Fujimori, Sachi. "Pink's 'Funhouse' Tour Stops at MSG."*Bergen Record*. October 3, 2009. Retrieved January 13, 2010 (http://www.northjersey.com/arts_entertainment/music/Pinks_Funhouse_tour_stops_at_MSG.html).

Harrison, Shane. "Sound Check: Thinking Pink: Bold, Brash Singer Likes to Stand Out—So Don't Expect Her to Shut Up Any Time Soon." *Atlanta Journal-Constitution*, July 20, 2006.

Majewski, Lori. "A Softer Shade of Pink." *Women's Health*, January/February 2010, pp. 40–43.

Montgomery, James. "Pink: The World's Most Underrated Superstar." MTV.com, October 7, 2009. Retrieved November 11, 2009 (http://www.mtv.com/news/articles/1623246/20091006/pink.jhtml).

Moody, Nekesa. "Back On! Pink Reconciles with Ex Corey Hart." HuffingtonPost.com, April 27, 2009. Retrieved January 13, 2010 (http://www.huffingtonpost.com/2009/04/27/back-on-pink-reconciles-w_n_191821.html).

Moss, Corey. "Pink to Play Janis Joplin in Movie About Her Life." MTV.com, April 2, 2004. Retrieved January 11, 2010 (http://www.mtv.com/movies/news/articles/1486154/20040402/story.jhtml).

The National. "Heart on the Record Sleeve." November 6, 2009. Retrieved November 11, 2009 (http://www.thenational.ae/apps/pbcs.dll/article?AID=/20091107/MAGAZINE/911059984/1284/rss).

Oldenburg, Ann. "Pink: There's Something About Me and Carey." *USA Today*, June 1, 2009. Retrieved November 11, 2009 (http://content.usatoday.com/communities/entertainment/post/2009/06/67515833/1).

Pareles, Jon. "Step Right Up." *New York Times*, October 6, 2009. Retrieved November 12, 2009 (http://www.nytimes.com/2009/10/07/arts/music/07pink.html?_r=1&scp=1&sq=pink%20and%20step%20right%20up&st=cse).

Petruso, A. "Pink." *Newsmakers 2004 Cumulation*. Detroit, MI: Gale, 2004.

RollingStone.com. "Pink Channels Janis Joplin." Retrieved January 16, 2010 (http://www.rollingstone.com/artists/pink/articles/story/6054633/pink_channels_janis_joplin).

RollingStone.com. "Pink Fights the Power." Retrieved January 16, 2010 (http://www.rollingstone.com/artists/pink/articles/story/5938439/pink_fights_the_power).

Vineyard, Jennifer. "Pink Would Rather Fall Off a Car Than Get Glammed Up for Her Videos." MTV.com, December 21, 2005. Retrieved November 19, 2009 (http://www.mtv.com/news/articles/1519101/20051221/pink.jhtml).

Wigney, James. "Pink's Happy to Reveal Herself." *Sydney Sunday Telegraph*, October 12, 2008. Retrieved November 16, 2009 (http://www.dailytelegraph.com.au/news/sunday-telegraph/pinks-happy-to-reveal-herself/story-e6frewt9-1111117725416).

INDEX

ABOUT THE AUTHOR

Lyn Sirota is a Pink fan. She is the author of several books for children and teens and lives in central New Jersey.

PHOTO CREDITS

Cover, pp. 1, 4 Michelly Rall/WireImage/Getty Images; pp. 3 (top), 26 Dave Hogan/Getty Images; pp. 3 (center), 31 Jeff Kravitz/FilmMagic/Getty Images; pp. 3 (bottom), 16–17 Frank Micelotta/Getty Images; p. 5 Jeffrey Mayer/WireImage/Getty Images; pp. 8, 10 Kevin Mazur/WireImage/Getty Images; p. 14 SGranitz/WireImage/Getty Images; p. 18 Valerie Macon/Getty Images; p. 20 Charley Gallay/Getty Images; p. 23 AFP/Getty Images; p. 29 © AP Images; p. 34 PhotoNews International, Inc./FilmMagic/Getty Images; p. 37 Getty Images.

Designer: Nicole Russo; Editor: Bethany Bryan; Photo Researcher: Karen Huang